The Eastern Around London

A COLOUR PORTFOLIO

KEVIN McCORMACK

Ian Allan

Above: Also preserved, in this case in Britain, is 'A4' Pacific No 60007 *Sir Nigel Gresley*, seen here near Ruislip, Middlesex, hauling a lightly loaded special organised by its subsequent owners, the A4 Locomotive Society. The date is 23 October 1965, and the train is heading for Paddington along the Western Region's Birmingham line. The locomotive returned to Scotland to continue working Aberdeen–Glasgow expresses until withdrawal in February 1966. *Author*

Right: Take a close look at this Standard 4-6-2 at Liverpool Street station, because it's not a 'Britannia'! Between 10 September and 21 October 1958 light Pacific No 72009 *Clan Stewart* was trialled on the GE line in anticipation of some of this class being part of a triangular exchange involving 'Britannias' and 'Royal Scots' aimed at providing more firepower for the London Midland Region. However, the GE, having accelerated its timetables on the basis of Class 7P locomotives, did not take kindly to a '6P' locomotive that was scarcely more powerful than a 'B1' and quickly sent it packing! *Roy Hobbs*

Previous page: Nowadays preserved in North America, 'A4' Pacific No 60008 *Dwight D. Eisenhower* hauls a down Leeds express between Potters Bar and Brookmans Park on 29 June 1957. *Ken Wightman*

First published 2009

ISBN (13) 978 0 7110 3338 2

Published by Ian Allan Publishing

an imprint of Ian Allan Publishing Ltd, Hersham, Surrey KT12 4RG

Printed in England by Ian Allan Printing Ltd, Hersham, Surrey KT12 4RG

Code: 0901/B

Visit the Ian Allan Publishing website at www.ianallanpublishing.com

Introduction

This is the fourth and last in the 'around London' set of colour albums, of which the first three have already covered the Western, Southern and London Midland in the 1950s and '60s, concentrating mainly on steam traction.

The London & North Eastern Railway (LNER) was the largest of the 'Big Four' companies created by the Grouping on 1 January 1923 of the numerous main-line railways that had existed hitherto. Three constituents of the LNER had served the capital, these being the Great Northern Railway (GNR), which operated the East Coast main line to Scotland and North London local services out of King's Cross station, the Great Eastern Railway (GER), which provided main-line services to East Anglia and an extraordinarily intensive network of local services to East and North East London out of Liverpool Street station, and, finally, the less than great Great Central Railway (GCR) to the Midlands out of Marylebone.

Inevitably, it is the lines out of King's Cross that dominate any nostalgic recollection of the Eastern around London, largely on account of the superb Pacific locomotives designed by the LNER's first Chief Mechanical Engineer, Nigel Gresley (who had held a similar position on the GNR). These locomotives included *Flying Scotsman*, the first steam locomotive officially to exceed 100mph, and *Mallard*, which holds the world speed record for steam — 126mph. Pacific design continued under Gresley's successors, Thompson and Peppercorn, but, thanks to the onset of main-line dieselisation, the latter's highly successful 'A1s' sadly did not enjoy their expected life span of 30-40 years and were lucky to achieve 15 years of service. Furthermore, none escaped the scrapman's torch, so, by popular demand, another one has been built, No 60163 *Tornado*, the first newly constructed standard-gauge main-line steam locomotive since 1960.

Steam working ceased at Liverpool Street in September 1962 but clung on at Marylebone until September 1966. King's Cross officially bade farewell to steam in June 1963, but it was a most impressive finale, largely due to the enthusiasm of the legendary shedmaster at King's Cross 'Top Shed', Peter Townend, who kept his stud of express locomotives spotlessly clean.

My own experiences of the Eastern around London during the 1950s and early 1960s (my schooldays) were largely confined to the East Coast main line, because I used to travel annually from London to Edinburgh to visit my grandmother and uncle, invariably by means of the 'A4'-hauled non-stop 'Elizabethan'. I always asked to go up on the footplate upon arrival, and on one occasion at King's Cross the driver of No 60011 *Empire of India* told me that our fastest speed had been 96mph, which I thought very exciting.

I also have a vivid recollection of Liverpool Street station, this being the sound of 'chuffing' engines. I would run along the concourse to look for the arriving locomotive and a potential 'cop' only to find up against the buffer-stops an 'N7' tank on a local service or station-pilot duty, the noise coming from its Westinghouse pump.

I am most grateful to the photographers who have provided their precious colour transparencies, none of which (I believe) has been published previously. The contributors I must thank are: Michael Allen, Bruce Jenkins, Geoff Rixon, Roy Hobbs, Nick Lera, Jim Oatway and John Cramp. Photographs taken by Ken Wightman are included courtesy of David Clark, those by W. C. Janssen and Marcus Eavis courtesy of the Online Transport Archive, and those by Frank Hunt courtesy of the Light Railway Transit Association (London Area).

Kevin McCormack
Ashtead, Surrey
September 2008

60060
60060

Left: Class A3 Pacific No 60060 *The Tetrarch* is prepared for duty at Top Shed in September 1961. Despite being fitted with a Kylchap double chimney, in March 1959, this locomotive ran until withdrawal in September 1963 without receiving the German-style smoke deflectors which were meant to be fitted to all 'improved' Class A3s. *Ken Wightman*

Above: Bursting out of Hadley Wood North Tunnel *c*1960 is Immingham-based 'B1' 4-6-0 No 61379 *Mayflower* at the head of a King's Cross–Grimsby/Cleethorpes train. Some 59 members of this class of 410 carried names, this particular locomotive being named in 1951 to commemorate the link between Boston, Lincolnshire, and Boston, Massachusetts, USA. *Mayflower* was the name of the ship that carried the Pilgrim Fathers to America in 1620. No 61379 was built in 1951 and withdrawn 11 years later. *Ken Wightman*

Above: Although through trains ran from North Woolwich to Palace Gates (Wood Green) most services were short workings between North Woolwich and Stratford (Low Level). On 24 June 1961 Class N7 0-6-2 No 69670 has just arrived at North Woolwich with the 12.18pm from Stratford. London City Airport now occupies an area of the former Royal Docks seen in the background. *Michael Allen*

Right: Also on 24 June 1961, Class N7 No 69640 is seen between Custom House and Canning Town with the 1.40pm from North Woolwich to Stratford. The train is running alongside Victoria Dock Road, passing the site of Tidal Basin station (closed during World War 2). The tall building in the background is Fyffes' fresh-fruit warehouse, while the sidings on the right belong to the Port of London Authority (PLA). *Michael Allen*

Peppercorn 'A1' Pacific No 60130 *Kestrel* coasts up the slight gradient between Brookmans Park and Potters Bar at the head of the up 'Yorkshire Pullman' on 29 June 1957. The 1928-built Pullman cars were replaced by new stock from 1961, the old carriages being transferred to the Southern Region. The 'Yorkshire Pullman' continued to run until 1978. *Ken Wightman*

Like the Peppercorn 'A1s', the Thompson 'B1' 4-6-0s were a wasted resource, unable to achieve an economic lifespan due to the Modernisation Plan, which often made no allowance for the age of the locomotive. In this view No 61367, heading a down Cambridge train near Potters Bar, sports new bolts on its smokebox-door straps, which are as yet unpainted. *Ken Wightman*

LIVERPOOL St
26

Left: Electrification of the line from Liverpool Street to Shenfield — a distance of 20 miles — commenced in the1930s, but completion was delayed until 1949 due to World War 2. On 11 May 1954 the photographer obtained a cab ride from Shenfield to Liverpool Street in an electric train and was able to capture this photograph of a sister unit. *W. C. Janssen / Online Transport Archive*

Above: Photographed [illegible] May 1954 from the cab of the same Shenfield electric unit, a train of empty stock snakes its way out of Liverpool Street station behind 'N7' No 69699. On the extreme left can just be discerned a surviving platform from the erstwhile Bishopsgate Low Level station, which had closed in May 1916. *W. C. Janssen / Online Transport Archive*

Above: The Royal Tr[illegible] handsome ex-LNWR [illegible] (No 77) dating from 1901, gr[illegible] [illegible]inshed at King's Cross, com[illegible]

Right: The signalbox on the platform at King's Cross station features in many photographs, but its interior will be less familiar. This view dating from June 1963 shows the track layout: the long mai[illegible] [illegible]forms, the shorter suburban platforms and, at the top and bot[illegible] down 'widened lines' to Farringdon and Moorgate. *B*[illegible]

KINGS CROSS

Above: Until electrification was extended beyond Shenfield to Chelmsford and Southend-on-Sea, in 1956, services between Liverpool Street and these further destinations remained steam-hauled. On 11 May 1954 one such train is about to leave Shenfield behind Stratford-based 'K3' 2-6-0 No 61830. This class, designed by Gresley for the GNR, consisted of 193 locomotives built between 1920 and 1937 and, when introduced, had the largest boiler [illegible] of any British locomotive type. *W. C. Janssen / Online Tra*[illegible]*hive*

Right: Built by the GER to replace the diminutive Holden 0-6-0Ts (later LNER Classes J67 and J69) on suburban services to and from the capital were A. J. Hill's 0-6-2Ts (LNER Class N7), of which 134 were constructed between 1914 and 1928. In keeping with GER tradition this example, No 69671, photographed at Enfield Town on 27 August 1960, has had its smokebox ring stripped back to bare metal and burnished. *Michael Allen*

ENFIELD TOWN

69499

Left and above: No fairies at the bottom of this garden, just trains! Seen at Bowes Park in the mid-1950s, Gresley 'N2' tank No 69499 heads an evening train on the Hertford loop while a freight train passes by. The 'N2' class, introduced in 1920, formed the mainstay of suburban services into and out of King's Cross until the onset of 'dieselisation' in the late 1950s, represented here by the Cravens diesel multiple-unit pictured at Enfield Chase, also on the Hertford Loop, in 1959. *Frank Hunt / LRTA / Marcus Eavis / Online Transport Archive*

Above and right: King's Cross (Top Shed) closed on 15 June 1963, coinciding with the official ban of scheduled steam operation south of Peterborough imposed from the start of the summer timetable. These photographs were taken six weeks earlier, on 4 May 1963. Pictured first on the replacement turntable installed in September 1961, Class A1 No 60120 *Kittiwake* proceeded to join an impressive line-up comprising, from left to right, 'V2s' Nos 60854 and 60817, 'A4' No 60032 *Gannet* and 'A3' No 60110 *Robert the Devil*. *Jim Oatway*

60817
1F 55
60120

L
42
61203
61203

Left: Liverpool Street is a hive of locomotive activity in this view featuring a surprisingly clean 'B1', No 61203. Although 410 'B1s' were built, the maximum number in stock at any one time was 409, one (No 61057) being damaged beyond repair in an accident at Chelmsford in 1950, before the class was completed. *Ken Wightman*

Above: Identifiable by its unique smoke-deflectors, the pioneer 'A1', No 60113 *Great Northern*, approaches Wood Green in August 1957. This locomotive was a 1945 Thompson rebuild of the first Gresley Pacific, No 4470, dating from 1922, although precious little of the original was reused. *Ken Wightman*

61607

Left: In 1945 Thompson began rebuilding Gresley's three-cylinder Class B17 4-6-0s as two-cylinder locomotives with 'B1'-type boilers, whereupon they became Class B2. On 7 October 1958 one of these, No 61607 *Blickling*, attached to a North Eastern Railway tender, is seen entering Bethnal Green station with a down Cambridge train. *Ken Wightman*

Above: In the London area the 'A2s' were seen less frequently than the other Pacific types. This class of 40 locomotives included four different sub-classes, No 60523 *Sun Castle*, captured at Hitchin in September 1958, being one of 15 'A2/3s' of Thompson design, built 1946/7. *Bruce Jenkins*

D5520
OXFORD 20'9
SOUTHEND 5'3
COVENTRY 14'9

Left: Some 263 Brush Type 2 (Class 31) diesel-electrics were built during the period 1957-62, and a handful are still running today. The first of the production batch, D5520, stands at Stratford station at the head of a train composed almost entirely of elderly Gresley coaches. The driver seems to be surveying the locomotive's undercarriage. Maybe all is not well! *Frank Hunt / LRTA*

Above: Following his untimely death in 1941 Sir Nigel Gresley was succeeded by Edward Thompson. Although the latter's Pacifics were not particularly successful, his versatile 'B1' 4-6-0s certainly were. No 61286 visits the London Midland Region on 10 May 1958 as it calls at Bletchley on its way from Cambridge to Oxford on the cross-country inter-varsity line which, apart from the Bedford–Bletchley section, has since been abandoned, although it may yet rise from the ashes. *Marcus Eavis / Online Transport Archive*

The start date for electric operation of the services from Liverpool Street to Enfield Town, Chingford, Hertford East and Bishops Stortford was 21 November 1960. Old lamps are giving way to new in this view, recorded a few months earlier, of Class N7 No 69664 at Bush Hill Park, the last station before the terminus at Enfield Town. *Marcus Eavis / Online Transport Archive*

Almost certainly the last Eastern locomotive to work a normal service into London, 'B1' No 61306, running an hour late, trundles through Harrow-on-the-Hill station on 23 August 1966 with the 8.15am from Nottingham Victoria. It was being trialled prior to its intended use on the last day of GC through services on 3 September 1966 but was failed on arrival at Marylebone; the 4.38pm return working was taken over by the only locomotive available, Standard '9F' 2-10-0 No 92228, which, much to the disgust of the crew, had reversed light-engine all the way from Banbury, apparently being too large for Marylebone's turntable! Sadly No 61306's incapacity, whilst not terminal, rendered it unavailable for the GC's last day, but it survives today in preservation with the *Mayflower* name bestowed originally upon sister locomotive No 61379 (see page 5). *Bill Piggott*

The Class B16 4-6-0s designed by Raven for the North Eastern Railway could sometimes be seen on the GCR's London Extension on freight or parcels trains, but on 14 October 1962 No 61438 was caught at Marylebone on railtour duty. Of the 70 locomotives of this class, built between 1919 and 1924, 24 examples, including No 61438, were rebuilt between 1937 and 1947 with new cylinders and valvegear, requiring higher running-plates. In 1949, to make way for new 'B1s', the first 10 built were renumbered, adopting the identities of withdrawn ex-GCR 'B9' 4-6-0s. *Ken Wightman*

A Cambridge–Liverpool Street train snakes round into Bethnal Green station behind Class B2 (formerly Class B17) 4-6-0 No 61615 *Culford Hall*. Of the 73 'B17s' only 10 had been rebuilt by the time the conversion programme was abandoned, in 1949, upon receipt of yet more new 'B1s'. All the 'B2s' would be withdrawn in 1958/9. *Ken Wightman*

Above: In this 1959 scene at Edgware the shunter is putting the single-line token into the ground frame to release the points, thereby enabling 'N2' No 69536 to leave the goods yard with the daily freight. Passenger services on this ex-GNR branch had been withdrawn on 11 September 1939 to enable it to be electrified as part of LT's Northern Line, but in the event only the short section from Finchley (Church End), now Finchley Central (cue for a song!), to Mill Hill East was electrified. *John Cramp*

Right: Having arrived at the terminus with the 5.10pm service from North Woolwich, Thompson Class L1 2-6-4 tank No 67716 runs round its train at Palace Gates (Wood Green) on 6 April 1962. The somewhat grandiose footbridge reflects the fact that the GER had built this 2¼-mile branch from Seven Sisters in the vain hope of attracting visitors to nearby Alexandra Palace, which the GNR already served directly with its own branch. Indeed, Palace Gates was optimistically built as a through station but did not technically cease to be a branch until 1944, when it was connected to the erstwhile GNR, enabling through working of freight and excursion trains. *Michael Allen*

67716

Above: The electric overhead is in place, ready for the replacement of steam-hauled trains on the Chingford branch, which split from the GE Norwich (via Cambridge) line at Clapton Junction. Class N7 No 69621 has just brought an up Liverpool Street train into Hackney Downs station on 27 August 1960. This locomotive, built at Stratford in 1924, has been preserved. *Michael Allen*

Right: German-style smoke-deflectors did nothing to enhance the appearance of Gresley's Class A3 Pacifics but were considered necessary to provide clear vision from the footplate following the fitting of a double chimney — a small price to pay, perhaps, for the extended life on top-link duties which these locomotives were consequently able to enjoy. Here a spotless Top Shed 'A3', No 60039 *Sandwich*, sets off from King's Cross with the 1.15pm to Leeds in January 1963. *Roy Hobbs*

60039

This page: Hatfield is the location of these two King's Cross-bound trains, pictured on 30 July 1960. Class A4 No 60013 *Dominion of New Zealand* creates a fine sight at speed, demonstrating why these locomotives were nicknamed 'Streaks'. Titled trains were by no means the preserve of Pacifics, and Gresley's powerful Class V2 2-6-2s were very competent performers on express duties, for which they were frequently used, as evidenced here by No 60983, the last of the class of 184, at the head of the 'Scarborough Flyer'. *Geoff Rixon (both)*

Above: Another spotless Top Shed 'A3', No 60044 *Melton*, takes on water at Langley troughs, between Knebworth and Stevenage, on 5 August 1962. The locomotives which eventually formed the 'A3' class were built between 1922 and 1935, but their BR numbers gave no indication of age; No 60044 was one of the earliest, from a batch built in 1924/5, whereas No 60039 (page 33) was one of the last, dating from 1934. *Bruce Jenkins*

Left: On the morning of 14 January 1963 the media were invited to Top Shed to witness Class A3 No 60103 *Flying Scotsman* being prepared for its final run in BR ownership (the 1.15pm from King's Cross to Leeds) as well as to interview and photograph its new owner, Alan Pegler. The locomotive hauled the train as far as Doncaster, where it proceeded into 'The Plant', its birthplace in 1923, for restoration. *Nick Lera*

Right: The eye-catching English Electric *Deltic* diesel demonstrator has just arrived at King's Cross in this view dating from April 1960. Built in 1955 and somewhat trans-Atlantic in appearance, due chiefly to its large central headlight, *Deltic* was initially trialled on the London Midland Region before moving to the Eastern Region in January 1959. Within a couple of months it was putting in fine performances, on one occasion reaching a top speed of 105mph, and as a result of its success an order was placed for 22 production locomotives for the East Coast main line. In 1961 one of *Deltic*'s twin power units expired, and in 1963 English Electric donated the locomotive to the Science Museum, where it remained on static display for many years, but it is nowadays to be found at the National Railway Museum's annexe at Shildon, Co Durham. *Geoff Rixon*

Withdrawn in September 1961, the last survivor of a class of 81, 'B12' 4-6-0 No 61572 was the subject of a successful preservation appeal. On 5 October 1963 it was used on a railtour from Broad Street station; this photograph was taken the following day inside Willesden roundhouse. Constructed by Beyer Peacock & Co in 1928 to a Holden GER design of 1911, the locomotive was rebuilt by Gresley in its present, large-boilered form in 1933. *Geoff Rixon*

Following displacement by diesels on suburban workings out of King's Cross, withdrawal of Gresley's 'N2' 0-6-2Ts, which originally numbered 107, started in earnest in 1957. The last 13 were withdrawn in 1962, among them No 69568, depicted at Harringay on 14 April that year. Most of the class, including this example, were fitted with condensing apparatus and short chimneys for working on Underground lines to Moorgate. *Michael Allen*

90409

Left: Much neglected by photographers, the Austerity 2-8-0s performed sterling work on the Eastern Region; indeed, 200 had actually belonged to the LNER, having been purchased by the company from the War Department in late 1946 and forming the 'Q7' class. A further 533 were purchased by BR early in 1949, among them No 90409, seen hauling a train of hopper wagons near Brookmans Park. *Ken Wightman*

Above: The introduction on 7 July 1958 of a German-built diesel railbus on the Audley End–Bartlow line, which was previously 'N7'-operated, was an attempt to render services economically viable but failed to prevent the withdrawal of passenger trains with effect from 7 September 1964. A few weeks before closure a service beyond Bartlow, to Haverhill on the Stour Valley line, leaves Saffron Walden, Essex. *Marcus Eavis / Online Transport Archive*

Left: The most numerous type built for the GER was Worsdell's 'Y14' (LNER 'J15') class of 0-6-0, comprising some 289 locomotives constructed over a period of 30 years from 1883 (and withdrawn over an even longer period — 42 years — starting in 1920!). Here No 65476 makes a spectacular departure from Epping with a special on the LT Central Line to Ongar on 28 April 1962.
Nick Lera

Right: This view at King's Cross on 19 April 1963 features a locomotive which should require no introduction. Withdrawn six days later and therefore making possibly its last revenue-earning journey in normal traffic, Class A4 No 60022 *Mallard*, holder of the world speed record for steam traction (126mph), unusually uses the crossover between Platforms 7 and 8 to reach its carriages.
Geoff Rixon

MALLARD
60022

Above: Hauling the 12.58pm train from Stratford to North Woolwich, Class N7 No 69640 ascends the gradient out of Connaught Tunnel to reach Silvertown station on 24 June 1961. When the Royal Albert Dock opened, in 1880, the GER branch was routed over a swing-bridge, but, as this would have resulted in unacceptable delays to trains, the tunnel was built, and the 'high level' route seen on the left passed to the Docks company (later the PLA), the GER retaining access rights in the event of an emergency. *Michael Allen*

Right: On 18 March 1961 Class L1 No 67737 pulls out of Custom House, between Canning Town and Silvertown, with the 12.58pm from Stratford to North Woolwich as Class N7 No 69709 arrives with the 1pm from North Woolwich to Stratford. Lines to Beckton (gas works) and Gallions (PLA) joined the North Woolwich line at Customs House. Today the Docklands Light Railway (DLR) station is situated alongside the cocooned North Woolwich line station, services having been withdrawn on 9 December 2006. Unlike so much in this picture, the tall building on the left remains extant today. *Michael Allen*

E87023E

Above: Class J69 No 68619 was a much-cosseted machine, serving from 1948 until its withdrawal in 1961 as a Liverpool Street station pilot. Built in 1904, it is seen shortly before its 1959 repaint in GER blue. When new this class formed the mainstay of Liverpool Street suburban services, nicknamed 'Jazz Trains' because of the yellow and blue stripes that used to be painted under the carriage roofs to denote First- and Second-class compartments, in order to speed up boarding. *Ken Wightman*

Right: Heading into Gas Works Tunnel at King's Cross to reach Top Shed, 'Deltic' diesel-electric No D9020 *Nimbus* was the penultimate example of its type to be built, entering traffic in February 1962. The 22 production 'Deltics' (later Class 55) were intended to replace no fewer than 55 Gresley Pacifics, and they performed impressively until ousted by HSTs. All were withdrawn in the period 1980-2, this example being one of the first two to be condemned, in January 1980; however, six were preserved, and in recent years some of these have reappeared in regular main-line service. *Jim Oatway*

M2
D9020

Above: Designed for London suburban services, Thompson's Class L1 2-6-4 tanks could be seen at all three Eastern Region main-line London termini. One such locomotive is depicted here on 2 August 1958, soon after leaving Aylesbury Town on an up local service to Marylebone on the former GC line. *Marcus Eavis / Online Transport Archive*

Right: Until 2 January 1960, when through expresses on the GC line ceased, there were two titled trains serving Marylebone — the 'Master Cutler' and the 'South Yorkshireman'. The latter ran to Bradford via Loughborough and Sheffield, Gresley V2 No 60831 being seen near Aylesbury at the head of a down working in the last summer of operation. *Marcus Eavis / Online Transport Archive*

THE SOUTH
YORKSHIREMAN

Above: The ubiquitous Thompson 'B1' class was constructed over a 10-year period between 1942 and 1952. Here No 61187, dating from 1947, is seen preparing to leave Marylebone on 13 July 1957 with a train for Manchester. *Marcus Eavis / Online Transport Archive*

Right: Class J15 0-6-0s were regular performers on the GER Cambridge–Colchester (Stour Valley) line, but this representative, No 65469, was photographed on 6 May 1962 working the annual amateur engine-driving and -firing special for Cambridge University Railway Club, which used part of the line for this activity. The train is seen at Haverhill, not to be confused with the Colne Valley line's terminus at Haverhill (later renamed Haverhill South). *Roy Hobbs*

HAVERHILL
CU RC
65469
3
J-15.

On 8 June 1963, exactly one week before the official end of steam at King's Cross, Top Shed could still produce a clean Class A3 Pacific. In this unusual view across the station towards St Pancras, No 60061 *Pretty Polly*, like all but five of the 'A3s' (as well as some 'A1s', 'A2s' and 'Deltics') named after a racehorse, is departing with the 10.25am to Peterborough. *Bruce Jenkins*

Right: Demonstrating once again that, despite being designed for high-speed freight trains, Gresley's powerful Class V2 2-6-2s were frequent performers on passenger duties on the East Coast main line, No 60899 hauls a train of at least 11 carriages near Potters Bar over the 1963 Whitsun holiday weekend. *Bruce Jenkins*

Right: Liverpool Street station in 1948, with LNER teak (unpainted) stock much in evidence. In apple-green livery is newly built Class L1 2-6-4 tank No E9008. When delivery was underway it was decided to number the class of 100 in a new series starting at 67701 (rather than 67700, as might have been expected), and consequently this example later became No 67709. *C. Carter*

Left and right: Class J69 0-6-0 tank No 68556 has the privilege of being shed pilot at Stratford on 8 September 1962, the final day of steam operation. The engine is not rostered to haul an express train, despite the position of the lamps; to spare crews the need constantly to change front and tail lamps, one of each colour (white and red) would be placed at each end of the locomotive. On the last day several locomotives had already been dumped out of use, including the 'J15s', 'J69s' and 'L1' seen here *(right)*, along with an elderly tender still bearing the initials 'LNER'. *Roy Hobbs (both)*

L N E R
65445

60144
KING'S COURIER
60144
3A33

Left and above: On 30 June 1962 Class A1 Pacific No 60144 *King's Courier* and a Brush Type 2 diesel await departure from King's Cross with their respective trains while Class A4 No 60003 *Andrew K. McCosh*, with burnished nameplate, reverses past the locospotters on Platform 1 to take the 3.55pm to Leeds. The Top Shed-based 'A4' had its moment of glory 12 months earlier, when, along with two other examples, it was selected to haul trains carrying Royalty and VIPs to the Duke of Kent's wedding at York, diesels apparently being regarded as too unreliable! *Geoff Rixon (both)*

61011
WATERBUCK
61011

Left: The Thompson 'B1' 4-6-0s were sometimes referred to as the 'Antelope' class, 40 of the first 41 built being named after these fast animals; unlike the Pacifics, they were insufficiently prestigious to be named after racehorses. With 'A3s' being given names like *Pretty Polly*, this may have been a blessing, although the 'B1s' managed to compete with names like *Bongo*! Unpronouncability of names was another aspect that racehorses had in common with antelopes, although No 61011 *Waterbuck*, seen at Aylesbury in 1961 at the head of a Marylebone-bound train, was an exception. *Marcus Eavis / Online Transport Archive*

Above: A regrettable omission from the ranks of preserved locomotives is of a 'Claud Hamilton' 4-4-0, this being the GER's principal express type until the arrival of the more powerful 'B12' 4-6-0. Claud Hamilton had been Chairman of the GER in 1900, when the first example of the original design (which became LNER Class D14) was built, and this was duly named after him. Later locomotives and rebuilds (LNER Class D15) had Belpaire boilers. Most examples of both versions were ultimately rebuilt with larger boilers (Class D16), but No 62613, seen at Stratford, its birthplace, in March 1959, was one of the final 10, built thus in 1923. The last surviving 'Claud', it would be withdrawn in October 1960. *Jim Oatway*

60505

Left: Possibly the rarest picture in the book — a clean 'A2/2'! The six locomotives of this sub-class were built by Gresley in the years 1934-6 as Class P2 2-8-2s for the demanding Edinburgh–Aberdeen line and rebuilt as Pacifics by Thompson in 1943/4. Neither incarnation was regarded as particularly successful, and as 'A2s' the locomotives were generally unloved and neglected. However, in this view No 60505 *Thane of Fife* looks quite impressive as it heads an up express near Brookmans Park. *Ken Wightman*

Above: The down 'Scotch Goods', an express fitted freight, is pictured on 29 June 1957 between Potters Bar and Brookmans Park in the capable hands of Class A4 No 60006 *Sir Ralph Wedgewood*. This locomotive was originally named *Herring Gull* but in 1944 took the name of the former LNER General Manager from another 'A4', less than four years old, which was damaged beyond repair in an air raid on York shed in 1942. *Ken Wightman*

69681

Left: Seen from the station's one-time taxi-cab entrance, which provided a popular vantage-point for locospotters, is Class N7 0-6-2 tank No 69681, serving as Liverpool Street station pilot in the autumn of 1958. Above the retaining wall in the background is the signalbox guarding the North London Railway's terminus at Broad Street, which would close in June 1985 to make way for the Broadgate development. *Roy Hobbs*

Above: The ex-GER line from Epping to Ongar was transferred to London Transport on 25 September 1949, becoming part of the Central Line, but was operated by BR until it was electrified, Tube trains taking over with effect from 18 November 1957. There is no sign of the conductor rails in this view of two trains headed by Class F5 2-4-2 tanks at Ongar. *Ken Wightman*

The 2.8pm train from Stratford to North Woolwich approaches Canning Town on 24 June 1961 behind Class N7 No 69692. The two tracks on the left now form part of the LT Jubilee Line Extension, a barrier having been erected between the pairs of tracks to carry electrical equipment, but the sidings on the extreme left, like the block of flats in Manor Road (right), have been consigned to history. *Michael Allen*

Ivatt Class C12 4-4-2 tank No 67352 might seem a strange choice for the Noel Park (Wood Green) railway exhibition of 13 September 1958, but this type, of which 60 were built between 1898 and 1907, was the mainstay of King's Cross suburban services until replaced in the 1920s by more powerful 'N1s' and 'N2s'. 'C12s' also made a brief comeback in the capital in 1948/9, when they were used on King's Cross–Alexandra Palace services. However, despite the efforts to make No 67352 look brand new, it was withdrawn only a few weeks later, when the class became extinct. Regrettably it was not preserved, unlike the locomotive to which it is seen coupled, 'J52' No 68846. *Marcus Eavis / Online Transport Archive*

On the last day of services on the Palace Gates (Wood Green)–Seven Sisters section of the line, Brush Type 2 diesel No D5666 prepares to leave North Woolwich for Palace Gates on 5 January 1963. The Italianate station building seen in the background, dating from 1854, became a museum dedicated to the history of the GER, having been replaced by a new station building in 1979 as a result of the revitalisation of services. This included electrification, enabling services from Richmond over the former North London Railway to be diverted from Broad Street to North Woolwich in 1985. However, the line was closed in 2006 following the extension of the DLR, which has stations very close to those at Silvertown and North Woolwich; there are plans to reopen the section from North Woolwich to Custom House as a heritage line, although this may ultimately fall foul of the Crossrail project. *Marcus Eavis / Online Transport Archive*

This view from the cab of a Shenfield electric features a spotless Gresley Class B17 4-6-0 hauling empty stock through Bethnal Green station on 11 May 1954. Constructed between 1928 and 1937, the 73 'B17s' were intended primarily to supplement the 'B12s' on heavier passenger trains, although the later examples were allocated to the Great Central. Postwar, 10 were rebuilt as 'B2s' (see pages 22 and 29). Bethnal Green was the site of Britain's worst civilian disaster of World War 2, no fewer than 173 people being crushed to death as they descended the steps to the Underground station in order to shelter from an air raid in 1943. *W. C. Janssen / Online Transport Archive*

Left: Stratford-based Class F5 2-4-2 tank No 67193 propels an LT Central Line push-pull train out of Epping towards Ongar. The 30 members of this GER class were rebuilds of Worsdell 'M15s' (LNER Class F4) constructed between 1903 and 1909 and were introduced in 1911. The Epping–Ongar line closed in September 1994 and was purchased from LT with the intention of running commuter services but, as yet, this has not happened. Instead, heritage steam services are likely to be introduced; the line has already seen limited diesel operation, and there is a possibility that a new 'F5' steam locomotive may eventually be built. *Bruce Jenkins*

Right: The line to Palace Gates diverged from the Liverpool Street–Enfield Town line at Seven Sisters. Intermediate stations were to be found at West Green and Noel Park & Wood Green, but both have since been obliterated, the site of West Green station, seen here, now being occupied by a school and sports centre. This view, recorded on 25 April 1962, features Class L1 No 67735 in charge of the 5.10pm service from North Woolwich to Palace Gates. *Michael Allen*

WEST GREEN

Above: At Thames Wharf Junction, passing over the site of a level crossing which once joined Victoria Dock Road (on the right) with North Woolwich Road, Class N7 No 69732 heads towards Custom House on 24 June 1961 with the 1.18pm train from Stratford to North Woolwich. The tracks to the left, known latterly as the Silvertown Tramway, belong to the original North Woolwich line, which was diverted to the north of Victoria Dock when the latter was constructed in 1855; a swing-bridge was provided for the old route, which passed to the Dock company (later PLA). The former public house on the right of the picture survives today (just). *Michael Allen*

Right: Framed between shunt and main-line signals, Class V2 No 60839 heads for Marylebone with an up Nottingham train on 3 September 1961. The locomotive's unkempt condition is typical of the GC at this time, while the Met carriages on the right help identify the location as Aylesbury Town. *Nick Lera*

60839

Above: It's back to the East Coast main line for this view of another Class V2, No 60905, travelling south between Brookmans Park and Potters Bar. The 'V2s' were often referred to as 'Green Arrows', because of the name given to the first of the class, but only eight of the 184 built were actually named. *Ken Wightman*

Right: The ever-versatile Thompson 'B1s' were a popular choice for inter-regional excursion trains. Here No 61158 has just passed through Kensington (Olympia) with the 12.32 service from Hastings to Manchester Piccadilly on 27 July 1963. *Michael Allen*

61158

GREEN ARROW
SILVER LINK

Left: Pioneers of their respective classes, 'V2' No 60800 *Green Arrow* (since preserved) and 'A4' No 60014 *Silver Link*, await the next call of duty at Top Shed. In 1935, as LNER No 2509, *Silver Link* captured the world steam record, achieving 112.5mph, only to have it snatched away the following year when another 'A4', No 2512 *Silver Fox*, reached 113mph. In 1937 the record passed to the LMS when Stanier Pacific No 6220 *Coronation* managed 114mph, but *Mallard* put it beyond reach in 1938. *Ken Wightman*

Above: Another view from the cab of a Shenfield electric on 11 May 1954, this time featuring a 'Britannia' Pacific, No 70038 *Robin Hood*, backing down from Stratford depot prior to hauling an express from Liverpool Street. The introduction of 'Britannias', with their '7P' power rating, brought a welcome acceleration of GE main-line services. *W. C. Janssen / Online Transport Archive*

Left: A grimy Class A2/3 Pacific, believed to be No 60520 *Owen Tudor*, heads a down evening train through Hadley Wood on 9 May 1963, during the last week of scheduled steam out of King's Cross. Whereas no 'A1' was preserved, an 'A2' survives, this being one of the later Peppercorn machines, No 60532 *Blue Peter*. *Roy Hobbs*

Above: The first standard-gauge steam locomotive to be preserved by an individual, GNR Class J13 No 1247 (latterly 'J52' No 68846 — see page 65), built in 1899, visits Ayot, on the now defunct Hatfield/Welwyn Garden City–Dunstable line, on 16 September 1961. The station building was burned down by a spark from a locomotive in 1948 and was never rebuilt, but the signalbox remained in use until January 1966. The line was lifted in 1971, and the area shown here is nowadays used as a car park for walkers. *Ken Wightman*

61141